Disaster SURVIVORS
Slammed by a TSUNAMI!

by Miriam Aronin

Consultant: Paul Whitmore
Director, NOAA's West Coast/Alaska Tsunami Warning Center

BEARPORT
PUBLISHING

ROCKFORD PUBLIC LIBRARY

Credits

Cover, © Mio Cade's Photography/Flickr/Getty Images, Peter Titmuss/Alamy, and Dan Barnes/iStockphoto; Title Page, © Peter Titmuss/Alamy and Dan Barnes/iStockphoto; TOC, © Chuck Babbitt/iStockphoto; 4, © AP Images/APTN; 6, © Kamarulzaman Russali/Reuters/Landov; 7, © Reuters/Landov; 8, © Horst Pfeiffer/epa/Corbis; 10, © Agence France-Presse/Getty Images; 12, Courtesy of Dr. Asha Pillai, Assistant Professor at St. Jude Children's Research Hospital in Memphis, Tennessee; 13, © Sucheta Das/Reuters/Landov; 14, © Punit Paranjpe/Reuters/Landov; 15, © Sipa Press/Newscom; 16, © Agence France-Presse/Getty Images; 17, © Beawiharta/Reuters/Landov; 18, © UNICEF Indonesia/Rachel Donan; 19T, © Gerald Herbert/Reuters/Landov; 19B, Courtesy of Dr. Asha Pillai, Assistant Professor at St. Jude Children's Research Hospital in Memphis, Tennessee; 20, © Kees Metselaar/Alamy; 21, © AP Images/Andy Wong; 22, © Hulton Archive/Getty Images; 23, Courtesy of the Pacific Tsunami Museum, Rod Mason photographer; 24, © Hugh Gentry/Reuters/Landov; 25, © Dadang Tri/Reuters/Landov; 26, © Daniel Templeton/Alamy; 27, © Jeremy Horner/Corbis; 28, © Bettmann/Corbis; 29, © Tatiana Morozova/Shutterstock.

Publisher: Kenn Goin
Senior Editor: Lisa Wiseman
Creative Director: Spencer Brinker
Design: Dawn Beard Creative
Photo Researcher: Daniella Nilva

Library of Congress Cataloging-in-Publication Data

Aronin, Miriam.
  Slammed by a tsunami! / by Miriam Aronin.
    p. cm. — (Disaster survivors)
  Includes bibliographical references and index.
  ISBN-13: 978-1-936087-48-8 (library binding)
  ISBN-10: 1-936087-48-0 (library binding)
  1. Tsunami—Juvenile literature. I. Title.
  GC221.5.A77 2010
  551.46'37—dc22
                        2009034574

For more information, write to Bearport Publishing Company, Inc., 101 Fifth Avenue, Suite 6R, New York, New York 10003. Printed in the United States of America in North Mankato, Minnesota.

122009
090309CGD

10 9 8 7 6 5 4 3 2 1

Contents

A Wall of Water

On December 26, 2004, carpenter Ari Afrizal was helping build a beach house on the Indonesian island of Sumatra. Suddenly, Ari and the other workers felt the earth shake. Scared, the crew moved away from the house and gathered nearby in the sand. Soon a wave about 3 feet (.9 m) high hit the house. A minute later, Ari and the others heard a loud whooshing sound. An even bigger wave was heading directly toward them. The gigantic wall of water hit the house and destroyed it. The water pushed Ari about 1,500 feet (457 m) **inland**, where he slammed into a mango tree.

Waves similar to this one hit the beach where Ari was working.

The second wave that Ari faced was 30 feet (9 m) high.

4

Ari was able to grab on to the tree. As he looked around, he saw that some of his coworkers were hanging on to other trees. "I thought the world was coming to an end," he said. Ari tried to hold on tightly, but as the huge wave returned to the ocean, he lost his grip. The powerful force of the giant wave, called a **tsunami**, swept Ari out to sea.

Indonesia

Pacific Ocean

SUMATRA

Indian Ocean

Islands that make up Indonesia

Arctic Ocean

Asia

Europe

North America

Atlantic Ocean

Africa

Pacific Ocean

Indian Ocean

South America

Australia

Southern Ocean

Antarctica

Sumatra is the sixth largest island in the world.

Adrift at Sea

Ari survived his first day at sea by grabbing hold of a wooden plank that he found floating in the water and lying on it. "The sun was hot," said Ari. "I had cuts all over my body." Still, he said, "I was not prepared to die."

Ari Afrizal

The next day, a tiny abandoned fishing boat floated near him. Ari climbed aboard. Even though it was leaky, it was better than the plank.

"I began to lose hope," Ari said. "But I was grateful to be alive." A week later, he found an empty raft and climbed onto it.

Ari's raft

While Ari was on the raft, he ate only coconuts that he found floating nearby. He used his teeth and a piece of wood to open the tough shells.

A Massive Underwater Earthquake

What caused this terrible disaster? One clue comes from the shaking that Ari felt before the tsunami hit. Scientists know that Earth's surface is divided into large sections called **tectonic plates**. When the plates meet, they can scrape or push against one another, or even break apart. These actions cause **earthquakes** and volcanic **eruptions**, which can eventually create tsunamis.

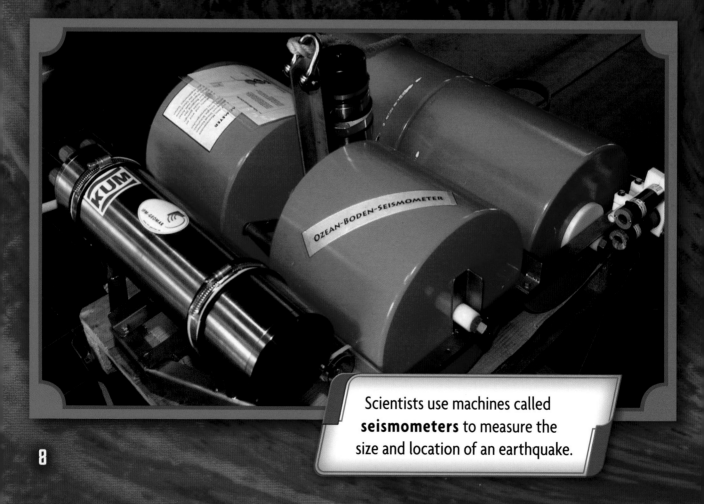

Scientists use machines called **seismometers** to measure the size and location of an earthquake.

On December 26, 2004, off the west coast of Sumatra, two plates tore apart, causing a massive underwater earthquake. Measuring about 9.1 on the **Richter Scale**, it was the most powerful earthquake the world had felt in 40 years.

Countries hit by the 2004 tsunami

THAILAND

INDIA

MYANMAR

Bay of Bengal

SRI LANKA

SOMALIA

Andaman and Nicobar islands

MALAYSIA

KENYA

MALDIVES

where the earthquake on December 26, 2004 took place

Sumatra

INDONESIA

TANZANIA

Arctic Ocean

Asia

Europe

North America

Africa

Pacific Ocean

Atlantic Ocean

Indian Ocean

South America

Australia

Southern Ocean

Antarctica

The tsunami affected many areas besides Sumatra. It hit parts of the Andaman and Nicobar islands, Thailand, Myanmar, Malaysia, Sri Lanka, India, and the Maldives. It also went as far east as Africa, striking mainly Somalia but also parts of Kenya and Tanzania.

A Humongous Wave

The 2004 earthquake in Indonesia pushed the ocean floor up and down for more than 700 miles (1,127 km). When this happened, a large amount of water was **displaced**. This caused waves to form and travel away from the area where the earthquake occurred.

Most tsunamis do not appear as walls of water like this one. Depending on wave size and location, some simply cause water levels to rise and fall several feet more than usual.

Tsunamis travel across the deep ocean very quickly. The waves move at more than 500 miles per hour (805 km)—about the speed of a jet airplane.

When a tsunami enters shallower water, it slows down and grows larger. The waves may grow to be very tall, creating a wall of water. That is what happened in many areas when the 2004 tsunami's deadly waves reached land.

How a Tsunami Forms

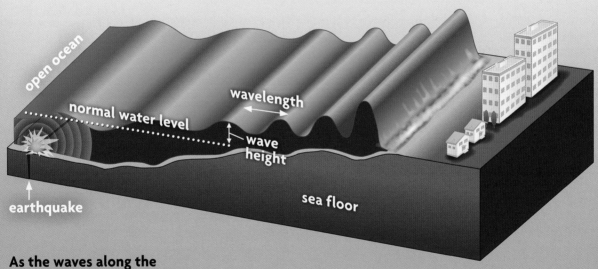

open ocean

normal water level

wavelength

wave height

sea floor

earthquake

As the waves along the rising ocean floor quickly pile up, they build into a huge tsunami that crashes onto the shore.

Scientists measured the effects of the 2004 tsunami around the globe. Water levels in the Pacific Ocean near the California coast increased by 16 inches (41 cm). Water levels in the Atlantic Ocean off New Jersey rose 13 inches (33 cm).

Horrible Destruction

Like Ari, Dr. Asha Pillai experienced the horrible destruction of the tsunami firsthand. Dr. Pillai was staying on India's Kerala coast, about 1,800 miles (2,897 km) from Ari's home in Sumatra. The building where Dr. Pillai was working was only about 30 feet (9 m) from the ocean.

On December 26, as she stood on her balcony, Dr. Pillai noticed that the ocean had pulled back, exposing more of the beautiful white sand than usual. Suddenly, a wall of water started moving toward the beach. Dr. Pillai watched helplessly as three giant waves struck the shore.

Dr. Asha Pillai is currently an assistant professor at St. Jude Children's Research Hospital in Memphis, Tennessee. She works with children who have cancer.

Water pulling away from the shore at an unusual time is a sign that a tsunami is about to occur.

"As each wave rushed forward, there was screaming and calls for help," she remembers. "People, vehicles, and plants were sucked like little toothpicks into the ocean."

Dr. Pillai was lucky. The highest water reached only to the bottom of her balcony.

Tsunami survivors clean debris from their damaged house in India.

Certain Death

About 1,000 miles (1,609 km) away from Dr. Pillai, G. Balan and his wife were also lucky to escape the deadly waves. However, their home and village in the Andaman Islands had been destroyed. They had nothing left, not even food.

To reach a rescue boat, they would have to walk 11 miles (18 km). There was only one problem: a **lagoon** full of crocodiles lay between the Balans and their destination.

The 2004 tsunami caused a lot of damage on the Andaman Islands.

The Andaman Islands are a group of islands located in the Bay of Bengal, which is part of the Indian Ocean.

"We realized that there was certain death on this side of the lagoon," G. Balan said. "We decided to cross and take the risk." Fortunately, the Balans made it to the boat. It carried them to a **refugee** camp where they would be safe.

A refugee camp in India

Struggling for Survival

Sadly, the Balans' experience was not unusual. The humongous waves of the 2004 tsunami had slammed into the coasts of many countries. Over 227,000 people were killed. Many of the victims lived in the region. Others were tourists who had come from all over the world to visit the area's beautiful beaches.

Tourists on Thailand's beaches fled the tsunami.

The tsunami destroyed many houses and businesses, too. More than one million people lost their homes and everything they owned. Many of them also lost close family members and friends. The **survivors** of the tsunami struggled to find food and shelter.

An elephant helps a survivor clear debris from houses destroyed by the tsunami.

In December 2004, about 290,000 people lived in the Indonesian city of Banda Aceh. About half of them were killed in the 2004 tsunami.

Helping Survivors

Those who survived the tsunami faced many difficulties. Some had serious injuries such as broken bones. Others became sick because they swallowed the dirty water brought by the waves.

Many survivors—especially children—also suffered from **trauma**. After losing their homes and loved ones in the waves, they were terrified and could not sleep.

After the tsunami destroyed her home and killed members of her family, Masyitah Sembiring (left) helped survivors in Sumatra stay healthy by making sure they had necessary supplies.

People around the world sent food, money, and medical supplies to help the people who had lived through the tsunami. The survivors helped one another, too.

For example, Dr. Asha Pillai used her skills to give sick and injured people medical care. She and other volunteers also worked with children who had survived the disaster to help them express their feelings through playing and art.

Former U.S. presidents Bill Clinton (third from left) and George H. W. Bush (second from left) visited Indonesia and helped raise money for the countries affected by the tsunami.

The U.S. government gave about $1 billion to help countries affected by the tsunami. Individual Americans and companies donated about $1 billion more.

A 12-year-old boy made this drawing to show what happened to his family in the tsunami.

Rescue at Sea

While other survivors crowded into refugee camps, Ari was still floating at sea. After two weeks alone, Ari finally saw a big ship approaching his raft. He waved his arms and yelled. "I looked up and saw people on the ship looking at me with binoculars," Ari recalls.

This beach near the area where Ari was swept out to sea, suffered severe damage by the tsunami.

The ship's captain was amazed to discover a survivor of the tsunami so far away from his home. Ari had floated more than 100 miles (161 km) across the open ocean!

The ship's crew gave Ari food, water, and a comfortable bed. Then they took him to a hospital where he recovered from his terrifying experience.

Ari (right) and another tsunami survivor recovering at a hospital in Malaysia

When Ari was rescued he was in the open sea about 75 miles (121 km) from land.

Tsunamis in History

The 2004 tsunami was one of the deadliest tsunamis in history—but it certainly wasn't the first. Tsunamis have been occurring since ancient times. The first one ever recorded happened about 4,000 years ago. Giant waves destroyed a **port** city in Syria, a country in Southwest Asia.

Records of tsunamis in the Indian Ocean are much more recent. In 1762, witnesses reported huge waves covering islands and coasts near the Bay of Bengal. River levels rose as far as 62 miles (100 km) inland from the coast.

In 1883, the volcano Krakatoa erupted. It caused a huge tsunami that hit the nearby island of Java in Indonesia. More than 30,000 people were killed.

In the Pacific Ocean, a major tsunami happens about once every ten years. One of the most destructive ones started with an earthquake near Alaska on April 1, 1946. About four hours later, giant waves began to slam Hawaii. The waves killed 159 people and caused about $25 billion in damages.

This photo shows the tsunami hitting Hilo, Hawaii, on April 1, 1946.

A Warning System

After the 1946 disaster, American scientists developed a system to protect people from tsunamis. It is triggered when scientists **detect** an underwater earthquake. If the quake has a **magnitude** of 6.5 or higher on the Richter scale, they observe the situation closely. Will a tsunami develop? If so, where might it strike?

The Pacific Tsunami Warning Center, shown here, is located in Hawaii and is one of two tsunami warning centers in the United States. The other one is in Alaska.

When scientists detect a possible tsunami or a major earthquake near the coast, they alert people who live in areas that might be in danger. Warnings may be sent by sirens, loudspeakers, phone calls, or announcements on radio or television.

Tsunami warnings save many lives. Before Japan started a warning system in 1952, 14 tsunamis had killed more than 6,000 people. Since the system started, only 486 people have died in these waves.

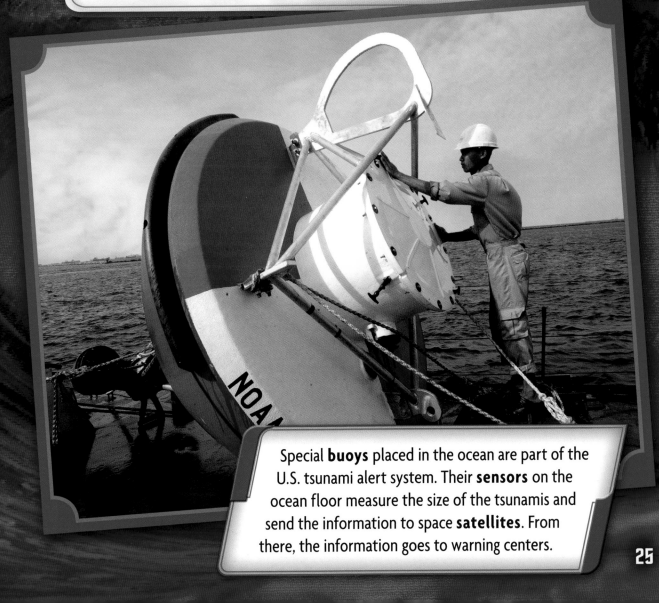

Special **buoys** placed in the ocean are part of the U.S. tsunami alert system. Their **sensors** on the ocean floor measure the size of the tsunamis and send the information to space **satellites**. From there, the information goes to warning centers.

More to Do

Unfortunately, the Indian Ocean region didn't have a warning system when the 2004 tsunami struck. However, scientists are working to change that.

Tad Murty is an expert on tsunamis. "There's no reason for a single individual to get killed in a tsunami," he explained. "The travel time for waves to hit the tip of India (during the 2004 tsunami) was about three hours. That's enough time for a warning."

Road signs like these show people where to go in case of a tsunami.

Along with warning systems, learning about tsunamis in school can save lives, too. A 10-year-old British girl visiting Thailand in 2004 had learned about tsunamis in geography class. While on the beach, she noticed the water had begun to form bubbles and turn foamy. She recognized this as a tsunami warning sign. By insisting that her family and others leave the beach, she saved many lives.

Scientists and emergency planners are working hard to improve warning systems. These new systems will help protect many more people from tsunamis. Hopefully, no one will ever have to go through the same experiences as the people affected by the 2004 tsunami.

Warnings can help people avoid being caught in tsunamis.

Famous Tsunamis

Throughout history, tsunamis have caused many deaths and major damage. Here are some of the most destructive ones.

Bay of Bengal, 1762
- On April 2, a giant earthquake struck the Myanmar coast.
- Witnesses later said that after the earthquake, "the sea washed to and fro several times with great fury." They described how rising rivers swept boats ashore and killed many people.
- Scientists believe this area is in danger of experiencing more serious earthquakes and tsunamis.

Japan, 1896
- On June 15, a massive tsunami hit the coast of Sanriku, Japan.
- Waves up to 100 feet (30 m) high slammed 175 miles (282 km) of the coastline. The water destroyed more than 9,000 homes and 10,000 boats.
- More than 26,000 people were killed. Many of the 5,000 survivors were badly hurt.

Crescent City, California, 1964
- On March 27, a tremendous earthquake struck Alaska.
- The powerful earthquake had 20,000 to 30,000 times as much force as a nuclear bomb. It caused a tsunami to form.
- Early the next morning, giant waves destroyed the entire business district of Crescent City, California. Eleven people there were killed.

Crescent City, California

Tsunami Safety

Here are some tsunami safety tips from the Federal Emergency Management Agency:

- ☑ If an earthquake shakes hard for 20 seconds or more and you're in an area near the coast, move 1 mile (1.6 km) inland or 100 feet (30 m) above sea level. Also, check for a tsunami warning.
- ☑ As soon as you hear a tsunami warning, move inland to high ground. Stay away from the beach. Never try to watch a tsunami come in.
- ☑ Water pulling away from the shore at an unusual time is one of nature's tsunami warnings. If you see this happen, move away from shore immediately.
- ☑ Save yourself—not your belongings.
- ☑ Stay away from flooded and damaged areas until officials say it is safe to return.

Glossary

buoys (BOO-eez) objects that float in a river or ocean to mark spots

detect (dee-TEKT) to find or notice

displaced (diss-PLAYST) moved things away from their usual location

earthquakes (URTH-kwayks) shaking of the earth caused by movements along a fault—a break in Earth's rocky outer layer

eruptions (i-RUHP-shunz) when volcanoes throw out hot lava and ashes with huge force

inland (IN-luhnd) on land, away from the water

lagoon (luh-GOON) a shallow pond separated from a larger body of water by a small piece of land

magnitude (MAG-nih-tood) size or intensity; earthquakes are measured by their magnitude on the Richter scale

port (PORT) a place where ships load and unload goods

refugee (*ref*-yoo-JEE) a person who must flee from his or her home because of dangerous conditions

Richter scale (RIHK-tuhr SKALE) a number system for measuring the strength of earthquakes; each increase of 1 point on the Richter scale means a 10-fold increase in ground shaking

satellites (SAT-uh-*lites*) spacecraft sent into space to send information back to Earth

seismometers (size-MAH-muh-turz) instruments that detect earthquakes and measure their power

sensors (SEN-serz) instruments that gather information about changing conditions such as heat, pressure, or sound

survivors (sur-VYE-vurz) people who live through disasters or horrible events

tectonic plates (tek-TAWN-ik PLAYTS) several large sheets of rock that make up Earth's outer layer

trauma (TRAW-muh) a terrible physical or emotional shock, or the effects of such a shock

tsunami (tsoo-NAH-mee) a wave, or a group of waves, caused by the quick displacement of a large amount of seawater, usually due to an earthquake, landslide, or volcano occurring underwater

Bibliography

Krauss, Erich. *Wave of Destruction: The Stories of Four Families and History's Deadliest Tsunami.* Emmaus, PA: Rodale (2006).

Lagorio, Christine. "Tsunami Survivor's 15 Days at Sea: Swimming, Drifting, Eating Coconuts—And Praying to Be Spared." www.cbsnews.com/stories/2005/01/11/world/main666238.shtml

Pillai, Asha. "Tsunami Survivor: Doctor Treats the Terrible Pain of Grief." *Stanford Report* (January 26, 2005). news.stanford.edu/news/2005/january26/med-tsunami-asha-012605.html

Rozell, Ned. "1946 Hilo Tsunami Survivor Shares Her Story." *Fairbanks Daily News-Miner* (May 17, 2009).

tsunami.org

Read More

Ingram, Scott. *Tsunami! The 1946 Hilo Wave of Terror.* New York: Bearport Publishing (2005).

Langley, Andrew. *Hurricanes, Tsunamis, and Other Natural Disasters.* Boston: Kingfisher (2006).

Morris, Ann, and Heidi Larson. *Tsunami: Helping Each Other.* Minneapolis, MN: Millbrook Press (2005).

Morrison, Taylor. *Tsunami Warning.* New York: Houghton Mifflin (2007).

Learn More Online

To learn more about tsunamis, visit
www.bearportpublishing.com/DisasterSurvivors

Index

About the Author

*Miriam Aronin is a writer and editor.
She also enjoys knitting, dancing,
and avoiding natural disasters.*